T0162676

PRAYERS

NO EXPERIENCE NECESSARY

Jo Therese Fahres

iUniverse®

PRAYERS
NO EXPERIENCE NECESSARY

Cover Art: "God's eye watching over us" by Clare Fahres Age 5

iUniverse books may be ordered through booksellers or by contacting:

iUniverse
1663 Liberty Drive
Bloomington, IN 47403
www.iuniverse.com
1-800-Authors (1-800-288-4677)

ISBN: 978-1-4917-7309-3 (sc)
ISBN: 978-1-4917-7310-9 (e)

Library of Congress Control Number: 2015912311

Print information available on the last page.

iUniverse rev. date: 07/31/2015

To Jerry,

Whose love for me and others
is a prayer in action.
Without his support, the dream of this book
would never have
become a reality.

Acknowledgments

My dream has always been to compile a book of prayers. No dream happens in isolation. It takes the love and support of many people to bring an idea into reality. I would like to thank the following:

My best friend of twenty-seven years, Cindy Bremeier, for her unselfish love and care for me, which I will treasure always.

Sister Jo Casey and the Poor Clare Sisters of Minneapolis, whose daily prayers and love have brought the healing of God and Our Mother Mary to me.

The Community of St. Gregory the Great Parish and School, the Pastoral Staff—especially Patti, Mark, and Diane, who support me in prayer and for the listening ear I need at times.

Father Thomas Demse, who is a true shepherd supporting me with daily prayers.

My sister Josie, my niece Nancy, and parishioners Cecilia and Rosie Posie, who were—and continue to be—my great cheerleaders as I continue my journey as a writer.

And to God, who blesses me every day with gifts and surprises that I will never be worthy of.

Table of Contents

Introduction

You are either a person who prays, or you are not. You either make the time to pray, or you do not. You believe in the power of prayer, or you think that prayer is useless. You understand what prayer is, or you've never had a need for it or an interest in praying.

Prayer has been defined as many things. The most common definition that we teach children is that prayer is talking to God. We use examples of friendship as we try to convey the message that God is our friend and that God is always there for us.

Depending on what generation you belong to, God hasn't always been seen as a friend. I was taught by the good Sisters of Notre Dame that God saw everything I did. God knew everything. If I was unkind to someone, and then tripped on the sidewalk, God was punishing me. If I spoke a curse word to my parents—besides having my mouth washed out with a bar of soap—anything that happened later that day was attributed to God letting me know I better change my attitude. God was to be feared, not loved. God judged everything we did, and one day we would have to account for everything we did.

Then, the Vatican Council II came along, and the ideas of who God is and how God relates to the people seemed to change. God wanted to be our friend. God wanted to be *my* friend. It was a struggle for me to come to accept that I was lovable, because God first loved me.

My prayer changed. Instead of prayers that started with the words "I want...", I found myself beginning to pray prayers of thanksgiving for creation. My meeting of Saint Francis and Saint Clare guided me to praise God in all things and all situations. Prayer became—for me—a way of life. Whatever I did, I found out that I could lift up to God in praise. The transition was long and hard as I tried to move towards loving a God that was tender, merciful, and kind. But, I made that transition.

When I am in need, I pray. When I am happy, I pray. When I am sad, I pray. When I am angry or frustrated, I pray. I place myself in the loving presence of the Creator God and ask for God's Divine assistance. Spirituality is who I am...my likes, my dislikes, my joys, my challenges. My spirituality and yours are rooted in the heart that God gives us. The call to love is part and parcel of our human existence. We are here to love. When we love, we experience a taste of the Divine happiness promised to us. When we refuse to love, we often find ourselves very unhappy.

This prayer book is the story of my life. It speaks of many different situations in life that I have encountered. These prayers reflect my search for wholeness. When you find yourself wanting to pray, but don't have the words to do so, I hope my own words will help you. I hope that my words will give birth to the words you already hold in your heart, and that—together—we can praise our loving God.

My prayer for you is that you will find hope and joy in these prayers, even the ones dealing with sadness and the need for healing. My prayer is that you will come closer to the God who made you, loves you, believes in you, and longs to be intimate with you. May you take the time for silence and not be afraid. In the quiet of your heart, may you find yourself in the loving embrace of the Creator who longs to be the center of your life. Let God into your heart. God is waiting for you. God bless.

Chapter One

Time for Quiet

Our world is very noisy. For many people, each day is a race, trying to get everything that needs to be done, done. The phone rings, someone knocks at the door, the television is blaring, and even our phones play tunes to let us know someone wants us. Our world is very chaotic.

Unfortunately, it isn't difficult to get caught up in all the noise. When it is quiet, we feel like something is wrong. When the children are silent, we become suspicious. Silence can be a two-edged sword. It isn't something we seek and something we often uncomfortable with.

It is in the silence that our hearts can be open to God. It is in the silence, we can listen to the intimate thoughts God wants to share with us. We must create a holy place—a sacred place—if we want to enter into this kind of intimate friendship with God. We must choose to make silence and be silent.

We all know that we can pray anytime we want to. With God, there is no time. Many of us use the morning and evening as natural times to acknowledge the presence of God. The prayers that follow are prayers that ask for the beauty of silence. In that asking, we can begin our day and/or end our day by praising the God who loves us.

Be Still

It is early morning, Lord.
Though I know this will be a busy day
I take these few moments to
quiet my soul and heart.

The sun is rising.
I see the flaming colors of your love,
and I ask that you might do the same to my heart.
Ignite my soul and mind so that I can enter into this day
with enthusiasm and peace.

Help me to use these moments of stillness
as a touchstone as I go about my day.
May all I learn in the stillness of these moments with you
be a source of strength in helping others to
experience the same.
Amen.

I Have No Time

Lord of All Time,
why is it that I so often feel like I have NO time?
Dazed as I am, I start my day hitting the ground running.
I never know what the day will bring.
It is hardly ever as I plan it to be.
I feel crunched for time.
I thank you Lord that you have time for me.
I thank you for taking the time to listen to me and my cares.

Lord,
Help me
to show the same courtesy to others who ask for a bit of my time.
Mellow me just enough to show that all are welcomed
into my time and space.
Slow me down enough to make the most of the time I share with others.
Thanks, Lord, for your time.
Amen.

In Silence

In the silence of my heart,
I hear your voice.
Unlike other times when
I struggled to know the meaning of
your words…
Now I hear you…
Calling me to a love so deep,
different than before.
I stop what I am doing and listen.
It is a call to be all that I am…
A call to offer with outstretched arms,
a return for the gifts you have given.
I pause…clearing away the
distractions and the noise I once
found refuge in…
I pause and let you into my heart.
I place the fear aside and listen.
Amen.

Blessed Silence

In the quiet of the night I hear you
whispering the words I need to hear.
My day filled with noise and
clutter.
Now it is quiet time for me
to be with you.

The silence at first frightens me but
my soul is calmed as my thoughts turn
to you and your love.
I can feel my heart relaxing in your
presence.

Your presence is sweet.
Your presence is rest.
In your calm and quiet, I am at peace.

Oh blessed Silence,
surround my heart
with your ever-present love and let me
bask in the beauty of your grace.
Amen.

Finally Quiet

It's quiet now.
And as I lift up in prayer,
those I love,
I think of all the blessings you've bestowed.
It was so hard to get going this morning.
But once I got moving,
I knew you were with me.
I had opportunities to see you, Lord,
in family and friends.
In the face of strangers,
You looked directly into my eyes.
You were with me.
You spoke through me.
You touched others using my hands.
You loved using my heart.
So it is no wonder that as this day closes,
and night has come, I am tired.
Yet, I am feeling so blessed as well.
So thank you,
for loving me,
for using me,
for trusting me,
to be your love today.
Amen.

Silence

Silence.
I find myself running from the silence because you are there.
You are in the quiet of my busy heart,
touching me ever so deeply yet with gentleness
as only a jealous God can do.

Silence.
At times a gift I can appreciate because the world has my head buzzing,
so rapidly that I can hardly hear myself think.
In that silence you whisper words of love.

Silence.
I need to meet you there more often, Lord.
A safe haven for my heart and soul,
the silence is a welcomed guest,
and most of all, are you.
Amen.

Sooooooooo Tired

Lord, you call me,
just as you called the prophets of old.
You call me
and I am not sure why.

I try to do the work you ask of me.
But, sometimes I get so tired.
It is hard to put one foot in front of the other.
It is as if each step is a workout in itself.

As I go about my tasks today,
be my inspiration.
Send a little extra energy my way
so that all I do is done
with a generous heart.

Give me a sense of zeal to love others and to move
beyond my own needs and wants.
Teach me to take the moments I need to rest
in your arms and be refreshed. Amen.

Night Prayer

Jesus,
Lord of life,
the day is over and I am tired.
I think about your days,
the preaching and teaching and healing
demanded of you.
Yet, you never failed to reach out to your heavenly Father.
You were granted grace and the presence of the Spirit.
Share the Spirit with me.
Do for me what the Father did for you.
I ask for the healing I need,
for rest of body, mind, and spirit so that
I may rise tomorrow with the energy to
serve you giving glory to God.
Amen.

What a Day

Lord,
this has been a day!
I am tired…so tired…I can't seem to see straight anymore.
Lots of people are seeking your face, Lord.
Show yourself to them.
It would make my job a lot easier.
They ask questions, Lord.
You know, a lot of people have lots of questions
about why some things happen.
I offer all their questions and hurts that I heard today.
There are many frustrations that come with trying to be a good person.
Hold us tonight, Lord, in your loving care.
Give all your people a peaceful night.
Thank you for all the gifts you have given this day.
Thank you for all the ways you have revealed your love.
Glory to you, Lord.
May each day be a day of praise and love.
Amen.

Thanks for My Yes

God of my life,
Thank you for the Yes I could say today.
Thank you that I could put myself first today and care about me.
Thank you for the joy I feel in knowing
I can take small steps towards larger goals.
Thank you for being God of my life.
Amen.

In the Mirror

When I look into the mirror,
Lord,
Let me see your face.
Let me be so much like you
that others will see
You in me.
Amen.

Looking for Good

Lord God,
I looked for you today.
You were hiding.
I prayed to see you.
Then you answered my prayer.
I saw a face with wrinkles that have seen the pains of life.
I looked and you were there.
His clothes were dirty, torn, and smelly.
I had no use for him.
When I looked beyond my prejudice,
You were there.
There was a child dying,
bruised and hurting.
I didn't know what to do,
but when I looked deeper into her eyes,
I saw you there.
You are here, God, in our world.
The single mom, the divorced, the homeless,
the poor, the unemployed, and forgotten
are all your children.
Help me to see with the eyes of my heart,
not just the ones in my head.
Help me to see and care.
Amen.

Chapter Two

The Gifts of Creation

When God finished making the world and everything in it, God said, "This is good." The sky, the ground, the birds, the animals, the trees, and all vegetation pleased God. Human beings, the greatest of his creations, pleased God the most.

People enjoy the beauty of the earth. Mountains call our names and say, "I am here. Climb me." Beautiful flowers give us the pleasure of their scent. Animals become close companions and fill the void of emptiness and hurt. The sun warms us and for those who love the snow, God provides beautiful scenery by gifting our trees and landscape with white from above.

It is natural for us to want to say thank you for all these gifts. Prayer avails us of the opportunity to do just that. The Creator is to be praised with our heart, soul and mind. This is our gift in return for all God has given us.

Along the Road

Journeying along the road,
at my own rate,
taking time to listen
to the Word of all Creation.
Sparrow sings a morning song of praise,
not new, but seldom heard before
I listened.

Looking to the distant hills,
wondering how high, how far away.
Wishing to be mountain bound,
I glance beyond the pebbled road I walk upon,
Heavenward,
and I can see.

Hungry for a food unknown,
thirsty for an everlasting spring,
well water, deep and still.
I long to taste of gentle streams and gurgling brooks
I know exists.

Time so scattered and lost,
so often lost,
by ignorance of what to do.
I pause now,
long enough to breathe the air,
surrounded by a love unseen,
I still myself! Until I feel.

I reach to sky and cloud and sun,
to touch the essence of their being!
Radiant of His face, I've seen before,
stretching high above my reach,
beyond my expectations.
I am lifted by the touch of Him who gives—
all good and powerful and loving.
I find I am created a new,
in His very image,
as I journey along the road.

Spring

Lord,
I was so excited when I woke up this morning.
The tree outside my window is budding.
I saw green for the first time in a long time.
The winter has been hard, and I have waited so long
for the breath of fresh air that comes with the seasonal change.

I feel hopeful again.
Create in me, O God, a spring awakening.
Help the inner growth that has been hidden for so long
sprout forth in me.
Help me be a sign of hope to others.
May this day be a day of praise to you.
Amen.

It's A Day

The sun is out,
the birds are chirping.
The sky is clear.
The wind blows gently over me.
It is a day to give thanks and praise.
Creator of our Universe,
thank you for the beauty of this day.
Thank you that you allow me to experience it
in all its fullness.
It's a day
where your goodness shines through.
Thank you.
Amen.

Challenges

Morning comes and once again,
I am challenged to start my day with hope.
My heart trembles
as I hesitate to even move from my bed.
I am safe here, under warmth of covers.
I am lying in the stillness of the early dawn.
I am safe
as a child resting in his mother's womb.
And I do not want to budge.
But reality calls me to start my day and
so I turn to you, Divine One, to hold me in your care.
As I rise from my safety zone,
help me to know that you rise with me.
Hold me in the very palm of your loving hands.
Help me to raise my heart and soul to you
in gratitude for this new day
regardless of what may lie ahead.
You are all I need.
You are my strength.
You walk with me.
Amen.

The Dance

The dance you call me to
goes round and round,
up and down,
across the stage of life.

A process,
that is so unpredictable one day to the next.
And you tell me that's okay.

Lord,
teach me to dance.
I want to feel the wind blow through my hair
as I twirl and reach for sun and sky.
Teach me your dance.

Capture my spirit with your Spirit
and turn me round and round
until laughter makes me sense
your true presence with me.

Lord of the Dance,
teach me your steps and help me to let you
take the lead.
Amen.

Morning

It's morning and every bone in my body aches.
I lie here, wondering why I need to get up.
It was a restless night and I am so tired.
I hear an inner call to rise.
You will be with me.
As I rise to meet the day,
I stumble as I wash and dress.
You will be with me.
I stop. I pray.
I ask for what I may need this day.
I feel your love and Spirit.
I am on my way.
You will be with me.
Amen.

One Day at a Time

One day at a time.
That's all I can handle.
One small step followed by another
is all I can manage to walk.

Difficulties come and I am afraid
that today will be too much for me to handle.
Then I remember
that one day at a time is what I have to give.
One day at a time is all that is asked of me.

In the moments when I feel
hesitant to move into the future,
help me to remember the present moment.
Help me to embrace the now.

Let your angels remind me that one day is like a thousand years,
and a thousand years is like one day with You.
Time is not my time, but yours.
You are pleased with my daily walk.
Help me to be pleased as well.
Amen.

Waiting

How I hate to wait.
How I long to have changes come quickly.
But that is not reality.
That is not the way life is.

Yet, you Lord, wait for me.
You are always waiting for me to come to my senses.
You are always waiting for me to admit the truth.
You are always waiting for me to open my heart to newness.

How I hate to wait.
How I long to have changes come quickly.
Give me patience, Lord.
Help me to believe that the changes that come will be real,
and lasting,
and in your timing.
Amen.

On a Clear Day

On a clear day, I can see forever.
On a cloudy day,
I am blind.
Blind to all the beauty that surrounds me;
blind to the love that hovers over me.
Blind to the world I am a part of.

On a clear day, I can feel the power of love.
I can look into a mirror and tell myself that I am good.
One a clear day, I realize that my purpose is
beyond any earthly goal.
That the divine calls me into being…always.

On a clear day, I can pledge to discover
more about the mystery I really am. My promise
is to meet the Divine in daily moments that
transcend the ordinary making all things
clear at last.

On a clear day, I am a different person,
Lord.
I am yours and only yours.
On a clear day, I am ready to do your will.
Amen.

Let Us Give Thanks

Let us give thanks to the Lord,
for all the Lord has done for us!

For the morning light that warms our hearts
with the love of God,
and for the ability to open our hearts
to the touch of God…

For the gift of being friends with others
and experiencing the laughter and joy
that relationships bring…

For the gift of our ministry that reaches to those in need,
and those seeking the Lord…

For the gift of leisure that calls us to refresh our souls,
by basking in the love of our God…

For the gift of the Spirit,
who challenges and calls us to be
the best that we can be…

For the gift of peace,
that Jesus longs for us to have and share…

We give you thanks, God of all creation,
for the gifts you give us.
Teach us as your children
to be open to your love and to the love of others.
We thank you and praise you with our
whole mind, heart, soul, and strength.
May all we do and say give glory to you.
Amen.

In the Light

I walk in light of day,
aware of true Love's calling.
I pause to hear God's voice
in the whisper of the breeze.
I am moved by the gentle love
of Lover still unseen.
I search the beauty of the world,
to catch a glimpse of God revealed.
How blessed am I to be considered
Daughter-Son of One on high.
How blessed to have Divine Touch
reach into the corridors of my being,
and to know the gentle Word made flesh,
again and again and again.
Love's calling, Spirit filled,
incarnation fulfilled.
In the light.
Amen

I've Walked a Mile

I've walked a mile or two today,
and I saw your face
in more than I would have liked to see.
In moments that felt hopeless,
at least to me,
I saw hope in the eyes of those who seemed useless,
at least to me.
Heart stretched by a touch of love,
a look of concern,
a glance of peace,
I was strengthened by their offering,
and I could continue walking
for another mile or two today.
I know that you walk with me.
That is all I need to know to go on.
Amen.

I Dance with God

I dance with God.
Early morning when the sun greets me.
My arms lift to heaven,
the blue sky blankets my vision.
I sing praise as the dance begins.

I dance with God,
as early birds sing their song high above me.
I join the swaying trees that offer praise,
as brother wind gently cradles
their branches and leaves.

I dance with God,
as I look at the faces of others,
angels in disguise anxious to begin their day.
I lift my heart and leap for joy,
for life has sprung forth anew,
and the dancing is a promise forevermore.
Amen

In Your Face

Lord of all creation,
we gather to thank you for the many gifts you give.
We ask that our eyes and hearts be opened
as we begin another day.

In your face, let us see love and joy.
In your face, let us see peace.
In your face, let us see our call to minister in your name.

Lord of all who walk with you,
We lift the hearts of all who hurt this day.
We ask that we have the grace to hold them tenderly
as we begin another day.

In your face, let us see the pain of others.
In your face, let us see compassion.
In your face, let us see our call to minister in your name.

Lord of all who search for you,
we ask for grace as we journey together.
Be our Eucharist and sustenance
as we begin another day.

In your face, let us see the hunger of those who search.
In your face, let us see bread that is broken and shared.
In your face, let us see our call to minister in your name.

Lord of all who come with outstretched hands and hearts,
reach down to us and lift our spirits in your love.
We ask that you,
who writes our names on the palms of your hands,
grasp us by the hand.
Assure us of your presence.

In your face, let us see hope.
In your face, let us see your faith in us.
In your face, let us see our call to love
as we minister in your name.
Amen.

Desert Song

Desert Song…
Played in the emptiness of my heart,
I wonder where you are.
Have you left me here in this
solitary desert place,
where no one comes nor can they come
to rescue me from the me within?

God of desert sands…
Where I see only dust and barren land,
blinded by wind,
disturbed by heat by day, and cold at night.
What can you do to save me from the depth of pain
I feel within this crumbling soul of mine?

Come, refresher of my soul,
caretaker of my heart,
redeemer of the lost ones.
Come, and open within my eyes
the mysterious flowers of desert song.
Show me the petals once more and bring me
the comforting arms of your garden oasis.

Sing with me the words of life, once upon my lips,
when all seemed right and beautiful.
Teach me the words… penetrate my heart with the
melody of grace.

Come to me, Lover of my soul,
embrace me with your tenderness,
and make me whole again.

Divine One, whom I call Father, Mother, Brother,
Sister, Friend,
come dwell with me and share this moment of desert hospitality,
where thirst and hunger are satisfied
by Your presence alone.
Amen.

Dance! Dance! Dance!

Dance a new dance,
ring round with God,
your partner and your friend.
Lover that God is
calls forth the depth of love
the energies of the Universe
created first in love.

The time is now.
The waters wait to purify.
The fires blaze to ignite
the wondrous gifts God alone has given.

Rise up!
Rise up!
Rise up!

It is time to
Dance! Dance! Dance!
With the God who sings the song!
Amen.

Morning Time

Good Morning, Lord.
The night was restless just as my soul
is restless when not in tune with you.
The sun beckons me to rise.
Before I do, let me take stock of what the day may be like.
If I forget to thank you for the gift of life…
If I forget to see you in the faces of others…
If I forget to praise you for the many gifts you give me…
I ask that you forgive me.
I ask that you remind me by tugging at my heart strings.
I ask you to be in my laughter.
Call me aside to remember that I would not even have this day,
if not for you.
Help me to spend this day mindful of your love and presence with me.
Thank you, Lord.
Now, I can face the day with courage and joy!
Amen.

God of Wonders

God of Wonders,
Maker of all that is good and beautiful,
I offer myself today to the service of your love.

Make me aware of the power of the healing
spirit that calls me to be who I am in your grace.
Awaken in me the movement of your
healing as I reach out to others.

Powers of love, greater than all things on earth,
raise me to a level of selflessness
that allows you to enter and fill me.
Deepen the rooting of your word in my heart.
With all the many gifts you give me,
never let me forget the humor you have placed in my
heart.

May laughter be my healing balm as I
continue to walk into the kingdom
of my deeper and truer self…sharing the
journey of life with others.

May the universe sing your song forever
and may I be privileged to learn the words
and sing it with my life.
Amen.

The Storm

I hear you in the storm.
As lightning flashes,
crackling against the deep blue sky,
Your voice rumbles as
the sound of thunder shouts
Your majesty and I am left to feel how
small I am compared to all the Universe.
I praise you in the storm,
raging out against my soul
and causing me to feel for just a moment or
two the fear of losing all in you.
I stand against the wind that blows new life into me,
taking in each breath,
though cold and damp and wet.
I stand tall knowing that I am rooted to the
earth that you have given us.
How blessed am I to be part of the song.

Amen.

Ojo de Dios
God's Eye

Ojo de Dios.
God's watchful eye,
watch over me.
Teach me to know
Your love and protection.
Teach me to see Your face in the ordinary events
of every day.
I thank You for earth, fire, air, and water that nurture life,
and pray that I may always give love and respect
to the world you give me to live in.
Teach me to treat our Mother Earth with tenderness and
love as we yearn to treat our brothers and sisters with compassion.
Heal us and protect us, today and always.
Amen.

Creation Prayer

Lord of All Creation,
who makes the rain and snow that waters the land,
who gives life to the wind and warms us with the brilliance of the sun,
fill our hearts with wonder at your creations.

Teach us to be wise as we use the resources of our earth.
Teach us to be realistic as we take upon
responsibility for the gift of Mother Earth.
Teach us to be wise as we discern the path you wish for us.
Teach us to be wise enough to call upon your
Spirit for help in our decision making.

Teach us to be ministers of knowledge as we both
learn and teach your Gospel to others.
Keep us close to your heart as we struggle to be
lovers in a world so often filled with hatred.
Teach us to be ministers of peace as we walk
and work with the people of God.

Bless us with understanding hearts as we listen
to the pain and sorrows of others.
Let our presence be a blessing to the hearts of those
we call brothers and sisters in your name.
God of all Power and Strength,
be for us the Way, the Truth, and the Life.
May all we do and say give true glory to You.
Amen.

Cold Rain

It is spring but the sky is gray and cloudy. The rain hovers
above and humidity is
waiting its turn to fall like blessed drops from heaven.

I haven't seen the sun for days.
My soul is stretched beyond belief as I try to trust that the
sun will shine again.

The cold outside and the cold inside of me greet each other.
Not with happiness and glee, but with understanding that
when one is present, the other is not too far away.

Son of God… sun of the universe, created for warmth and
fellowship with God, please shine on us.

Awaken the earth and flowers once again.
Awaken my soul as well and grant us the grace of your
presence.
Amen.

A Troubadour's Song

I am a troubadour of sorts,
wandering the empty streets
of my own heart.
I sing a song once given to me by You,
Divine Presence in my life.

Your hymn of praise filled with
Allelu and Sanctus
now become my own
as cross-backed I walk a dusty street
of loneliness.
Misunderstood and mocked,
misguided and deceived,
I long for truth that only You can offer.

My song continues in my soul,
struggling to come in tune with yours
as I search for peace.

And your song,
senseless to many,
now makes sense to senseless me
as I come deeper into knowing
the love you have for me.
Amen.

A Prayer of Thanks

Generous God, who gives us all that we need to follow your Son, Jesus,
we offer praise and thanks for this day.

We thank You for the warmth of the sun,
the light of the moon,
and the twinkling of the stars
in the heavens above.

We thank You for the changing colors of the trees
that recharge our souls and call us to a sense of beauty.

We thank You for the service you call us to.
We pray for the people You ask us to minister with,
and those we are called to serve
in the name of Christ.

We thank You for friendship and the joys of love.
We thank You that we can love
in your name.

We thank You for conflicts that call us to deeper dependence on You.
We thank You for the gifts of
forgiveness and reconciliation.

We thank You, God, for life and all that each day brings.
May we ever be grateful to You
for the gifts You give.
Amen.

Have I Insulted You?

Lord of My Life,
have I insulted you?

When I doubt myself and
the talents you have given me,
when I question whether I am worthy to
be called your servant,
does this insult you?

When I fail to share myself with others,
or refuse to volunteer because I am afraid,
does this offend you?

You are Lord of my life.
I lift to you my doubts and fears,
my false humility in denying your gifts to me.
I offer my confession and apology if I have insulted you.
Forgive me,
and give me courage to move on.
Amen.

Thank You

Where can I begin to thank you, Lord?
With every breath I take, I experience your power and love for me.
One glance at the sunrise, even on a cloudy day,
tells me you are Lord of All Creation.
As the day unfolds and I begin to meet others
and share their ups and downs,
I am aware of your spirit working around and within all of us.
How precious is your gift of love!
You come into our world to make it holy,
and ask us to share in your mission.
You gift us with the power of your Spirit so that
we can be holy messengers of your peace.
You trust us to bring the Kingdom of love into
this world so much in need of love.
Thank you for the trust you place in us.
Amen.

Chapter Three

On Healing

It hurts to hurt. When we fall and hurt ourselves, we can clean up the wound and bandage it up. Even though the hurt may sting and bruise, we know that eventually it will heal and we will be better. But when our hurt is emotional or spiritual, it is harder to come back to wholeness. The heart aches. The mind pulls up all kinds of past experiences and our soul is burdened with hurt that we can't always explain.

Many times we blame ourselves for what is happening around us. Although it may be true that we have participated in wrong doing, there is always more to the story than meets the eye.

Jesus experienced hurt. He was misunderstood by the people around him. He was judged by authorities. He was betrayed by his closest friends. Yet, Jesus continued to live his life as God intended him to. Jesus experienced our human condition to the fullest. Jesus needed healing.

The difference between Jesus and us is that Jesus knew where to go to be healed. The scriptures speak of Jesus seeking out lonely places to get his thoughts together and to pray. Jesus prayed. He sat in the quiet presence of God while he watched the waves of the sea of Galilee go back and forth. He prayed on the mountain top where he could view the various beauties of God's creation. When he returned to his ministry, he was filled with God's Spirit and could share that healing that he received from God, with others.

The following prayers are prayers for Healing. They are prayers that hopefully help you to raise your heart to God. My prayer is that together, we can pray for ourselves and what we need, and for all those who are in pain. Let us also remember to pray for our world that is in need of healing.

Alone

Alone in this place,
deep within my soul,
I hear the whimpering of a child.
She is frightened as she shivers in the dark,
wondering if light will dawn again.
She is wrapped in Teflon-like resistance,
allowing nothing to penetrate the part of her that hurts so deeply.
She sits alone.
She waits but doesn't really know what she is waiting for.
She cries, but isn't sure why the tears are so hard to release.
She weeps and as she weeps, her mind goes back to other times,
when her self-worth was minimized and practically forgotten.
She is there.
Simply there.
Not knowing what to do next.
She grasps for words to explain the feelings she is having.
There are none.
She is numb.
Yet she hopes that words will rise from her broken heart
and mending can occur.
She is numb, and yet there are moments when she wants to scream
in pain, praying for the light to break through her darkness.
She stands in the mystery of the darkness and reaches out,
grasping for someone or something to hold onto.
She feels a hand reaching out for hers.
She takes it and waits.
Filled with fear and hope,
she clutches onto the hand and prays.
The Savior is here.
I know the child is me.
I know the journey is mine.
I know the Savior is the light.
I am no longer alone.

A Prayer for all who Face Addiction

Divine One,
who loves me and calls me by name,
walk with me this day.
Take my hand as I journey into this new day,
full of challenges and choices.
Help me to choose the good.
Help me to choose life for myself so that
I may reflect the love and life you offer all
who seek the good and holy.
Be with me when I am afraid.
Be with me when I am tempted
to be less than what you call me to be.
I offer this day and all it holds to you.
Keep me safe and give me joy.
Amen.

Only You Can Heal Me

God,
heal me.
Heal my mind, that I may know of your love.
Heal my heart, that I may know of your presence.
Heal my body, that I may serve you well.
Fill me with energy, to love you.
Heal my arms, so I may reach out to others,
and help them carry their burdens.
Heal my legs,
strengthen them so I can walk the path
You show me.

God,
heal me,
as only you can,
and claim me as your own.
Thank you.
Amen.

Finding Peace

I've heard others say
peace comes when we are in harmony with the world.
I have no reason to doubt that, except that I don't feel it.
My heart longs to know the truth of life.
My soul longs to know the path to follow.
My spirit longs to reach to heights of inner solitude that
resides in the depth of my own person.

I cannot reach down into the core by myself.
I don't know how and I am afraid.
Angels of God,
journey with me into the valley of despair.
Guide me as I walk through my own valley of death.

Help me to die to self.
Help me to resurrect the joyful self that I know lies somewhere
in the bondage of fear and anxiety.

Transform my attitude.
Transform my fears into the glory of freedom.
With that freedom to be who I am meant to be,
help me find peace.
Amen

For Healing

Jesus,
heal me.
Hold my hands and move them to reach out to others.
Come, hold my mind.
Inspire me to think thoughts of you and love.
Hold my heart.
Fill it with energy to give love to others.
Heal me.
Give me the strength to walk the path you show me.

Jesus,
heal me as only you can.
My trust is in you.

Amen.

God of the Dance

O, God of the Dance,
embrace me in your arms and twirl me
round and round.

Help me to see all the beauty around me.
Keep my limited feet elevated by your strength and Spirit.
Be my Teacher,
showing me the steps I know and those I must learn.

In the moment of healing,
in your time,
set me down so I can dance
with your Spirit
and
in your love.
Amen.

God of Transitions

God of transitions,
bless our hearts and hold us in your love.

In the early morning,
as dawn breaks forth from darkness,
we offer ourselves to you
because we trust in your light.

As we make our way into our work day,
trying to remember all that must be done,
we walk without fear,
because we trust in the guidance of your Spirit.

Winter days linger,
and Spring attempts to break forth in glory.
We believe in beginning again
because you are a God of second chances.

The reality of death to self,
the sacrifices of wants and desires,
calls us to grow.
We embrace the earth in hope,
because you promise growth from the dying seed.

Our eyes, slightly opened, have more to see.
Our lives have more to absorb.
We celebrate the gift of life,
because you are the God of truth.

In our challenges, our ups and downs.
Our attitudes that need reforming,
we give you praise,
because you are a God who cares.

God of transitions,
bless our hearts and hold us in your love.
Amen.

Break Chains, Not Chairs

Gentle God,
I need your help.
I am so angry, I don't know what to do.
Sometimes I want to break everything in sight.
I am tired of the gossip.
I am tired of the back biting.
I am tired of all the useless energy that goes into hurting others.
It is so easy to get sucked into these devilish lures.
I am tired of sometimes being part of this.
These actions are life-draining.
Come, Gentle God,
and help me break these chains that hold me down.
Free me from the devil's tactics.
he tempts me to be less than who you created me to be.
You are kind, merciful, and loving.
Send your spirit so I may be the same.
Amen.

Watching Addiction

Lord God,
it's hard to watch one I love
give in to that which robs life.
The drugs, the drink, the food
that lures one into darkness,
changes the person I know.
The struggle is real.
The disease is real.
I sometimes feel so helpless.
I don't know what to do to help.
I don't know if I can help.
Help me to pray.
Help me to believe that prayer can help.
Give me patience and prevent me from
enabling destructive behavior.
I trust you are with me.
Thank you for your presence.
Amen.

An Addict's Prayer

God,
help me.
The forces of evil are all around me.
I drink, I shoot up, I eat,
all without control.
I am an addict.
I want to stop.
I need to stop.
Please give me the wisdom to admit
that I need help.
Help me to realize that I cannot do this alone.
I need support.
I need you, Lord.
Help me to want to turn my life around.
Teach me to choose the good.
I am here, Lord, I am here.
Please stay with me on this journey.
Amen.

The Jackpot

I walk into the casino, Lord, and I am a different person.
I leave my cares at the door and enter a wonderland filled with
sounds, color, and flashing lights.
Bells ring, people shout, and I know someone is a winner.
It is my fantasy land.
I honestly can say I never expect to win.
Breaking even is a thrill.
Even losing a little is okay, because I feel good.
I am refreshed.
Then I look around and I see those seeking for the jackpot.
They look for the win that will change their lives.
Some use rent money.
Some use food money.
Some don't know when to leave.
It isn't fun for them.
It is a battle.
Take care of those who need your guidance.
Help them to seek the help they need.
Help us all see that you are the only jackpot we need.
In your love, we are all winners.
Amen.

Hatred

I hate not being able to see who I really am.
I hate that there is nothing that cures my sadness.
I hate that I have so many wrinkles that there isn't
enough Botox to fill them.
I hate that I have a hard time losing weight.
I hate that I am not fulfilled by my job.
I hate that I am afraid to let people know who I am.
I hate that I am limited in my physical abilities.
I hate that I don't have the things others have.
I hate! I hate! I hate!
And, yes, there are even times that I hate the fact that I hate.

God of love,
enter me,
dispel the darkness,
remove the jealousy,
refresh my spirit with confidence
so that I can love.
Help me to believe love is everything,
and that you are with me always.
Amen.

He Didn't Just Sit There

He was on the ground,
in the midst of a large crowd, but quite alone.
He heard the shouts that You were coming by.
He didn't just sit there.
He screamed at the top of his lungs.
It was your name he cried.
You stopped.
You listened.
He wanted to see.
You granted his request.
Give me the grace to do what I need to do.
to be the person you want me to be.
Help me to shout your name and ask for mercy.
Help me to ask for the vision I need to see your face.
Please, Jesus,
don't let me give in to just sitting there.
Amen.

Lift Me, Jesus

The day is just beginning.
Yet, I am tired and worn.
Lift me, Jesus, in your loving arms.
Lift me and hold me close to you,
cheek to cheek like a mother,
cradling her baby.

I need to know your tenderness today.
I need to feel your embrace of unconditional love,
so that I can go on another day.

I am weak. You are strong.
I am needy. You are all I need.

So, lift me, Jesus, and help me to nestle in your arms
and feel at peace.
Amen.

Loneliness

I feel like everything is going on around me.
My heart aches.
I feel lost.
Yet, tears have not found their way
to my eyes.
Lord,
hold me, touch me,
be present to me as I sit here
feeling all alone.
Embrace me with the garment of
love and peace.
Hold my soul as only you can,
and lift me from my sorrow,
for you are my rock.
Amen.

Reaching

I know I need you, Lord.
My hand reaches…
but I am afraid.
Will You hold me close?
Grasp my hand?
Calm my heart?
Father, Mother, God,
Reach down to me as I reach out to
You.
Help me to trust You in every way.
Amen.

Searching for the Face of Jesus

Lord Jesus,
you show yourself to me in many ways and at
many times when I least expect to see you.
Open my eyes that I might see your reflection in
the faces of my brothers and sisters.
Open my heart that I might embrace each person with love
as I would embrace you with all my heart.
Open my hands that I might reach out to every heart
that cries for mercy and kindness.
Lord Jesus,
be my constant companion as I journey through this life.
Let me always be mindful of your hand,
embracing mine as I seek your face in all I meet.
Amen.

Tell Me

Lord God,
tell me I am good
when I feel bad about myself.
Tell me I am lovable
when I don't feel so lovable.
Tell me I am worth something
when I feel worthless.
Tell me that I am valuable and unique in your eyes,
when I feel ordinary.
Tell me, Lord God,
that as your created wonder, I am special
and give me the grace to believe you.
Amen.

Touch Me

Touch me,
with the gentleness of love,
Spirit-filled and kindly.
Hold my face in your own hands.

Touch me,
hold my tears in confidence,
my fears in your great heart,
my failings in forgiveness.

Touch me,
with compassion from your soul,
that I might feel the
goodness that is you.

Touch me,
deep within my soul,
and call to resurrection
the life you know is there.

Touch me.
Amen.

The Pause

Pausing for a moment,
amid the struggles of the day,
I visualize the coming
of the light of understanding.

Entering the crown
and resting in my thoughts,
I feel the presence of the
Divine in what was once simply human.

Embraced by love and comfort,
breathing slowly as I focus
on the presence of the God-head,
now, not far away, but here
with me, around me, in me.

I am full of thoughts of praise,
oneness that calms the fears
and calls me to peace once more.

The sky is dark,
and all I strain to see
is hidden in the cloak of black.
I look for stars,
sparkling diamonds above,
Heaven's windows.
yet from here, below,
I see only blackness.

Being of Light,
God of Light,
brighten the sky above me.
Help me to see the hope
You promise.
Help my soul to hold on,
not to despair, but to Your
Promise of life.
Yours are the only promises worth
cherishing…
The promise that light shall
dawn again,
and all will be well.
Amen.

Urn of Ash-White Hurts

I hold, within my urn of Ash-white hurts,
a quantity of little deaths of dreams not realized,
of visions not yet clear.

With cluttered heart I am before you,
wondering how I can do your holy will.

Watchful of what I pray for,
Afraid I might get what I ask,
I hesitate to say to you,
"Unbind me…declutter the inners of my soul."

I am afraid.
Not fully trusting your words of comfort,
"I am with you always."
I am afraid to step out in faith.

Reach out to me.
My hand is outstretched before you.
Reach out to me, and touch my urn of hurts.

Take the ashes of my life,
let your spirit rise again in me,
so I can soar like an eagle,
over ragged heights.

Hold my urn in your hands,
blow my hurts to the wind.
Create in me, through me,
a new vessel
to encase your love,
to hold your love,
to dispense your love.

You go before me always.
You go before me always.
You go before me always.
Help me to trust.
Help me to believe.
Help me to move.
Amen.

What's Next?

My prayer is one of frustration, Lord.
I just about get a handle on one thing and something else
becomes a challenge for me. What's next?

I hesitate to ask.
I don't mean to sound whiney, but you know a person can
take just so much. Every day, I feel as if I am fighting for
my life. I can do this… can't do that. I hurt here and ask for
healing. Then I find myself hurting somewhere else and
asking for more healing. Just as one area of my life seems
to be coming together, another begins to fall apart.
What's next?

If I sound frustrated, it's because I am.
There are times when I want to give up but I know in my
heart that isn't the solution. So I pray…and believe me,
sometimes that is really hard to do.

I know you are in control. If that's the lesson that you want
me to learn, please, I think I know it. I know that you alone
can heal me. I know that you alone can give me what I need
each day.

I need a space to feel safe for a while. Hold me in your
tenderness and let me lean against your breast. Put your
cheek to mine and whisper words of comfort.

Accept my prayer today and help me to move on,
even on those days when I am tempted to ask,
"What's next?"
Amen.

You are the Hands of God

You reach out to touch me and
power comes from you to me.
Your gentleness embraces
what pain I hold within.

You hold my face and cradle
my tears.
God's own hands hold me
through you.
You cherish me in a moment
when I feel afraid and lost,
and of no value.

Power comes from God,
through you
to me,
and energy flows as I begin
to ask for what I truly need.
Freedom.

Thank you God for a friend that leads me
to you, by loving me as I am.
Amen.

Chapter Four

Friendship

I have friends. I have beautiful friends. I have friends who make me laugh.

I have friends who sometimes make me cry, because they are hurting. I have friends who cry with me, because I am hurting. I have friends who are spontaneous. I have friends who need to plan every detail of a getting together evening. I am grateful that I have these people in my life.

I choose my friends very carefully. What I look for in a friend is a beautiful heart. I look for someone who is unselfish and giving. I choose someone who helps me to be the best that I can be. In return, I do the same for them.

I have always heard since childhood that Jesus wants to be my friend. This was easy to accept when everything seemed to be going well. When times got rough, I experienced some doubts about God's love for me. As I've aged, I have come to realize that even in my darkest moments, God has been with me.

These prayers about friends and life situations are meant to help the person reading this pray out of frustration, anger, or fear. These prayers are meant to bring to mind the joy that friendship can have. My hope is that you can find—in my words—the words of your own heart, and make them your own.

Friends

Thank you, Lord, for friends.
Each day, I meet situations that I think I can't handle.
Then, I remember those you give me who believe in me.
They trust in me.
They depend on me, and challenge me to keep going.
My friends are images of you.
They touch me with your hands of healing.
They console me with your words of encouragement.
They share your presence so that the pain isn't so bad.
They touch my heart because you have touched theirs.

Lord,
friendship is such a gift.
Help me to appreciate the friends I have, and
teach me to be a friend to others.
Help me, too, Lord,
to remember that you are my best friend,
and that because of you I am privileged
to have these gifts in my life.
Amen.

You Call Me Friend

You call me friend,
Lord of the Universe.
You lean toward me with compassion,
and call me to be calm.

Your greatness is more than I am able
to take in.
Your mercy, more than I deserve.
Your friendship, gift beyond all gifts.
Your love, a mystery to me.

Yet you call me to life.
Vibrant, ever moving, cup spilling over
with grace.
You celebrate me, long before I can even
fathom the person that I am,
and you delight in me just as I am.
You understand my journeying.
Most precious friend,
stay near, walk with, and come back with me.
Amen.

I Just Can't Love This Person

Lord,
I know you want me to love people.
But, to tell you the truth, there are some
people that just get on my nerves.
Either they are spending all their energy complaining about something,
or they sit back and criticize what others are doing.
They just aren't happy unless they're unhappy.
I don't get it.
We so often hear how short life is, and how
we should live it to the fullest.
You told us that.
And you also said we should love each other.
Even though I try to care about these folks,
I honestly don't care.
They drive me crazy.
I don't know what to pray for.
Patience? I don't know if I want to try again.
Compassion? I don't know if I care enough.
Tolerance? I don't know if I am strong enough.
I need to understand what it means to love.
In those moments when I want to turn my face
and heart from those you send my way,
stop me.
Remind me that I have clay feet and I am just as human as everyone else.
Help me to see that you died and rose for all of us.
We are all God's children, and we need to get along.
Lord, in those moments when I can't pray for what I should,
please send your Spirit to help me so I may be a true follower of yours.
Amen.

Clay Feet

I often hear how short life is,
and how I should be living it to the fullest.
There are times when I meet folks I just find difficult to love.

I have asked for patience, for compassion, for understanding.
I find myself falling into tolerance instead.
And I feel uncomfortable.

I have clay feet, Lord, and I need your help.
I am no angel.
Let me see in others the gifts they have to offer.
Adjust my attitude.

In those moment when I can't pray for what I should,
send your spirit to help me.
Help me to change.
Amen.

The End of the Line

Lord,
I am the youngest.
Always teased and treated differently.
Envied by older siblings.
I was always thought to be spoiled by my parents.
Although I often denied being treated in a special way,
as an only child,
I was the last of ten.
I realize now how true the spoiling was.
Today, I ask a blessing on my family
on earth and those in heaven with you.
Remind them of my love for them,
and keep me ever mindful of their love for me.
Amen.

Walking With Angels

Lord,
I walked with angels today.
I spoke with a man who was caring for the poor
by delivering food baskets and cleaning supplies.
So many things we take for granted.
I have a colleague that visits the sick and
is often present when they face death.
Her compassion is awesome.
I work with teachers who go beyond the 3 o'clock
dismissal time and work late into the evening for the good
of their students.
There is good in the world, Lord.
So often we only hear of the violence.
I pray for all the angels that are among us.
I pray for all who make a difference in the lives of others.
I thank you, Lord, for allowing me to walk with angels
and work with them for the glory of your name.
Amen.

Our Special Friends

Lord God,
Lover and redeemer of all your children,
I offer a prayer for your special children.
Their eyes may be different.
Their walk and speech are labored.
You, God, see them in your image.
You know the road may be more difficult for them,
so you give them bigger hearts,
shining smiles of steel and the purest love for life.
Some may say they are handicapped.
In reality, they are more in tune with love than many of us.
Protect our special brothers and sisters.
Be their guide and inspiration as they
inspire us to love the simple things in life.
May we learn to truly love as they love.
Thank you for the role they play in bringing your kingdom.
Amen.

A Different Day, A Different Read

Lord,
I am so confused.
Every day is different.
One day, my friend is happy and fun to be with.
The next day, she is short and sharp with her words.
I used to think to myself
"What have I done?"
Then I realized that it wasn't anything I had done.
At least, I was not aware of anything.
So Lord, I try to treat my friend with kindness.
I try to accept that I haven't walked in her shoes today.
I try to love her with patience and kindness.
But, I won't lie.
It's hard to do.
It's hard to accept.
It's hard to be silent when I want to attack back.
Be with me, especially when we are together.
Fill us both with the grace to be kind to each other.
I ask this in your name,
with confidence and trust.
Amen.

One Never Knows

I never know what seeds I sow,
what words I say or small acts of kindness I may do.
I never know what heart is touched and healed,
what spirit imprisoned in sadness is set free.
Lord,
help me to sow
the seeds of love
in ground that is rocky or sandy or fertile with love.
Give me strength to work for the kingdom,
no matter the cost,
knowing that you will nourish
whatever is planted in your name.
Amen.

Trusting Love

My mind recalls the fear within
as I placed my trust into your care,
being there, wondering about
the message God would give.
Rightfully grounded, shoes removed,
united with the energy of Spirit.
You call me to a trusting presence,
of Godhead, whom I have met before.

Being there, afraid,
yet wondering what to expect,
I felt the energy of God through
hands touching me, over me,
reaching into the very heart of me.
And, as tears welled up within me,
overflowing from deep within,
I felt my soul cry out for mercy.
As pain racked through my body,
I cried out for mercy.
As I came face to face with the touch of
God, holding, stretching, and loving me,
I felt mercy.
My heart and head reeling with emotion,
not knowing how to sort the inner struggle,
I was asked to let it go, to let it be,
to let it heal.

Sobs were my response as I felt my inner- self
go limp and ask for mercy.
I lay there in mercy... drenched in grace.
And even though my eyes were closed, I
could see clearly the face of God... I could feel the touch of God.
In a moment's embrace, it was safe.
In a moment's embrace, it was like
being home in the midst of darkness I had never known before.
And God was there. And you were there. And I was there.

Compassionate God,
Compassionate Friend,
in the safety of your touch and embrace
I have come to know your power as God in my life.
Thank you for your mercy, for the
revelation of your love and for the
forgiveness my heart seeks.
Amen.

Betrayed

Lord, I am feeling sad.
One I thought was a friend
has let me down.
I feel like Jesus when Judas
turned away.

Help me to move beyond the sadness
I feel in my heart right now.
Give me the courage to meet
with this person and make things right.
Help me to be open to misunderstandings
that may have happened.

Let me approach this person in love.
Please,
be with me.
I don't like how I am feeling inside.
I know you can help make things better.
Amen.

Unnecessary Slam

Lord God,
I need your help, right now.
My day has been going fine.
I'm feeling good and looking good as well.
I took care about getting ready, today.
Slapped a smile on my face for everyone.
I was determined it was going to be a great day.
Then it happens.
A wise remark from someone bursts my bubble.
I feel insulted, betrayed, and sad.
Lord,
why can't people keep their mouths shut if all
they want to say are negative things?
Don't they realize that words are like a sharp knife
that can cut and hurt if used unwisely?
Give me patience, Lord.
Lift me up beyond the insult and hurt I feel.
Let me continue to have a good day
and offer my hurt to you.
Keep me strong,
and help me to know who I really am.
Amen.

Laugh With Me

Laugh with me, Divine One.
Help me to see how foolish I am
when I try to be God.
Help me to see how fruitless it is to
spend my time and energy doing what
you are so much better at.

Laugh with me, Divine Presence in our world.
Help me to see the beauty of every
day and the funny side of every person.
Help me to enjoy the gifts they bring to this world
and teach me not to be envious.

Laugh with me, Wondrous mystery.
I tend to make big things out of little
things and many of these
don't concern me at all.
Help me to stay out of other people's
business.
Help me to realize that they don't need
me to help them solve their problems.
They have you.

I want to laugh, but sometimes I need
help seeing the humorous nature of things.
I want to enjoy the sunshine, the
sound of children giggling, a good joke
and the refreshing sense of the gentle winds.

Divine One,
tickle my soul if I am finding it hard
to laugh.
Bless me with a sense of humor and a
joyful outlook that cannot be wavered
by anything.
Amen.

Trust

Today, let me walk in trust
of the power of good over evil,
the power of love over hatred.

Today, let me believe
that this day can be different,
filled with meaning and joy.

Today, let me know that I am guided
by angelic light that shatters the darkness
and brings me to a sense of peace.

Today, let trust be the word
that moves me to respond to life,
and experience each moment as a gift.
Amen.

The Mountain Top

Come to the mountain top.
It's a deeper view from here.
Release my worries and fears.
Give me balance to stand strong.

Fill me with a song of joy and praise.
Create a sense of gratitude in my heart
for every gift you give.

Let me sing a song of hope.
Let me sing a song of love.
Let me live a song of praise.

Let today be a new day.
Let today be a new day.
Let today be a new beginning.
Amen.

Just A

Heavenly Father,
I pray today for all the "Just a's".
For all those who are
just a mom.
Just a dad.
Just a secretary.
Just a book keeper.
Just a teacher.
Just an aide.
Just an assistant.
Just a maintenance man.
Just a cook.
Just a store greeter.
Just a daily Mass goer.
Just a volunteer.
Help me to pray for them often.
Help me to help them realize they are all special gifts
to those who seek your love and kingdom.
bless them with energy to do their just a's jobs
with enthusiasm and love.
Most of all, help them to see that their
just a's jobs are more than a job.
What they do is real ministry,
And without them,
we would truly be less blessed.
Amen.

Transform Me

"And there, before their eyes, his face shone like the sun and
his clothes became white as light. Peter said, "It is good to be
here. Let me make three tents here, one for you, one for Moses,
and one for Elijah." And a voice was heard saying, "This is my
beloved Son, with whom I am well pleased, listen to him."
-Matthew 17

God of all creation, you gift us with life. Transform me.
God of mercy and reconciliation, you teach
us forgiveness. Transform me.
God of strength, you teach us endurance. Transform me.
Jesus, Son of God, you teach us to love. Transform me.
Jesus, Healer of All, you teach us compassion. Transform me.
Jesus, Shepherd of my heart, you guide us. Transform me.
Jesus, Bread for the journey, you feed us. Transform me.
Jesus, One who does miracles, you gives us hope. Transform me.
Jesus, Comfort of those who are tired, you give us rest. Transform me.
Spirit of God, Force of Love, you give us love. Transform me.
Spirit of God, Mindful of the Father's will, you
give us inspiration. Transform me.
Spirit of God, Whirlwind of Creativity, you
invite us to imagine. Transform me.

Father, Son, and Spirit, come to our assistance as we try to lead your
people closer to you. Fill our hearts with a sense of wonder and awe
at the miracles you work in our ministries every day. Help us to be
obedient to the dedication we have pledged to your church. Help us to
be supportive of each other. As Jesus was transformed on the mountain,
as a sign of hope of heaven to come, help us to be transformed as well
so that those we serve can experience in us the joy of serving you. Glory
be to you, God, Father, Son and Holy Spirit, both now and forever.
Amen.

Chapter Five

Loss

No one likes to lose. I don't like to lose. I would rather win at a card game, computer games, or any other competitive activity I am involved in. I don't like it when my team loses. I somehow feel cheated.

There are other losses that we as human beings experience. Relationships that go sour cause us pain. When a promotion goes to someone else, we may feel less valued. When the slot machine flashes GAME OVER, it can cause a sense of disappointment in us.

Loss is part of our human experience. We are all in the process of dying. Each day, we come closer to our final day. As we grow older, there are many things we can no longer do. These are little deaths, and are part and parcel of becoming aged. We become old and the parts of us that once were strong and healthy seem to gradually diminish. It takes longer for us to do a task. We don't remember as well as we used to. We can't hear as sharply as we could in our youth. Every time we lose something or someone, we are reminded of our mortality and for some of us, it's frightening.

The promise of eternal life is what can keep us going. This is not our home. We are on a journey. The journey is a road filled with rocks and obstacles that can discourage us. We need faith and trust. We need each other.

Uniting ourselves in prayer with others can bring us consolation. Understanding the pain of others can bring us to an awareness of what it means to be a part of the human family, and the family of God. Prayer is the gift we give to each other.

Taking a Holy Walk

We begin our walk with palm branches and cries of "Hosanna!" as we welcome you into our world. We praise you because we think we know who you are and why you have come into the world.

We sit with you as you take the bread and dip it, pass it to the one who will betray you, and we foolishly ask, "Is it I, Lord?" We question, ready to accuse each other of wrong doing.

We know that you are betrayed for thirty pieces of silver by one of your own. We never stop to think of the ways we betray you by our actions or lack of action.

We listen to you say the bread is your body, and the cup your blood. We hear the words, "Remember me." Yet we sometimes forget.

We see you wash feet as a sign of servanthood. So often we forget to offer hospitality to those who come to us.

We watch as you are lifted high in agony. We wait for you to show your power and redeem the world. We run from daily deaths because we are afraid.

We watch as you die, are brought down and given to your Mother. We watch and we wonder.

We wait as you are laid in the borrowed tomb. We wait, trying not to give into the fear that death can hold over us.

Jesus of Nazareth,
We declare you Savior.
Open our minds and hearts,
that we may truly know you.
Prepare us for the celebration
that your Resurrection offers us.
Keep us from fear and immerse us
in your loving kindness
so that we may be an extension of
the love God has shown to us through you.
May we celebrate in joy the Spirit of
knowledge and become together your
Easter people.
Amen.

Bread Broken

Christ,
Bread—broken.
Wine poured out.
You give life by giving us Yours.
Held high on the cross,
forgiveness on your lips,
you call us to bear the cross on
our foreheads and in our hearts.
Bread forever,
chalice of love,
take up your home in us.
Body of love,
blood of salvation,
be flesh of our flesh and
bone of our bone…
So deeply one with us
that we know without a doubt
you walk with us on this journey,
caring for us
as we walk along the road.
Amen.

Three Hours

Three hours,
Sacred Hours.
Your image on a cross.
I kneel before you,
Crucified Lord,
holding the nails of my sins.
Your death pays the price,
once, for all.
I thank you
for stretching out your arms,
for opening your hands,
for receiving my shortcomings,
for giving me forgiveness,
and the promise of new life.
Because of those three hours.
Amen.

You Are Mystery

You are mystery to my heart.
You are Awesome Love that knows no limits.
You come to me in Eucharist. Small, frail, yet you are Mighty God.
You allow yourself to be placed into my hands.
Awesome Mystery, you ask for Awesome Trust.
Jesus, Lord of the Great Thanksgiving,
you love me enough to give your all to me.
You only ask that I give my all to you.

Cup is poured out.
It is a sign of your blood life given for me.
I hold you in my hands and to my lips.
I drink of the cup of salvation.
Awesome Mystery,
you are awesome, God.
Jesus, Lord of the Everlasting Feast,
you love me enough to give your all to me.
You only ask that I give my all to you.
Amen.

This is My Body

This is my Body,
simple words you said so long ago,
and full of promises you become Lord—
visible—
small and helpless
held by human hands and hearts.
You are a mystery bound with love,
inviting us to eat and be IN MEMORY OF YOU.
You are the bread of Life,
of sun and storm,
smooth and rock filled miles.
Your taste is real,
your gift is simple,
your presence one with us.
Blessed are you,
Lord of All Creation.
Your goodness gives us this wine to drink.
Work of human hands,
symbolic of human hearts longing to be loved.
Your call to die to self brings us to accept the suffering
as we wait in hope for the kingdom to come.
Grounded and drained of life juices,
we come to your table
to receive the cup that gives us salvation.
Our hearts and bodies are renewed and refreshed
by the warmth of communal celebration.
Lord, you choose well the sign of wine.
It is proof that you want us to be happy.
As we come to eat and drink at this Eucharistic feast,
help us to see that you sanctify the struggle to be one in You.
Amen.

The Shepherd

S urely you know my name
H ugging my very soul
E ven in my darkest hours
P eace is what you offer me
H earing your voice gives me comfort
E ngaging my heart in love
R ealizing I am never alone
D esiring always to be your child.

Amen.

The Mystery

O Paschal Mystery,
suffering through death
to life again.
I enter, afraid,
that what I know—
all that is familiar—
will die.

Why fear what has already been
deemed alien to love?
Why walk in trepidation when
life seems round the bend?
Why hesitate, O fearful heart,
when the Divine invites?

Come, Soul.
Come, heart.
Come, spirit deep within.
Rise up and face the sun.
Bask in its warmth and
sing a new song.
Amen.

I Want an Explanation

Lord,
I want an explanation.
Why did you take the one I love so soon?
My faith is challenged by the events of the day.
My heart is filled with tears.
I search for answers for events I don't understand.
Lord, God of Mercy,
I ask you for your consolation and your peace.
Be with me as I try to understand
that your ways are not my ways.
Help me to trust that you are good for your promise that
one day, my mourning will turn to joy.
Be my companion in days to come,
and hold me gently in your love.
Amen.

The Crosses of Others

Lord Jesus,
the pain of your people cries out from the land,
and the cross of Calvary forms once again.
I know of the pain though I don't know the faces of the
lonely, unemployed, and those suffering from illness or emptiness.
I know of the hearts of many who live in
broken bodies and troubled minds.
Our world tries to yield its crosses to you, Lord,
hoping that you, who once bore the misery of humanity,
will touch us with your divinity.
We wait for you to increase our capacity to love,
that we might help each other carry our crosses.
We long to be your servants,
by serving one another.
Help us to bring healing and peace to our broken world.
Oh, Savior, helps us to love each other.
Amen.

Age Takes a Toll

Lord Jesus,
you loved your parents.
I love mine too.
Time has taken its toll.
The memory is fading.
What happened a moment ago fades into the past quickly.
The past soars forth, and is as clear as day.
Stories told once
are repeated over and over and over.
The knowledge of surroundings is faint.
Sometimes, I am a stranger.
Bless my aged parents, and hold them in your love.
Fill me with patience and understanding,
as well as a sense of duty to care for them as best I can.
Help me listen well,
even if I have heard the tale before.
They gave me life.
As they prepare to come to you,
help me to be resolved to make these years,
months,
or days
the best for them.
Teach me to see them with a grateful heart.
Amen.

Saying Goodbye

Creator God,
you give life to all creatures.
You form humans with soul and spirit
in your own image.
You give time to love, to share, to create
memories of love and adventures.
Then, you separate us.
Sometimes by misunderstandings.
Sometimes by distances.
Sometimes, even by death.
In the moments we are apart, please hold us
in your tender care.
Help us to see that you alone are the center of our lives.
You long to see us all be one again.
Be with us as we long to turn our
separations to embraces,
misunderstandings to compassion and acceptance.
Help us to realize that one day you will turn our
mournful goodbyes to joyous hellos, forever.
Amen.

Prodigal Judas

What made Judas turn against Jesus?
Was it the disappointment that the Kingdom
was not as he expected?
Was it a loss of hope that there would never be peace?
Was it that Judas could not see that love will overcome all evil?
How quick I am to judge this Judas,
who never seemed to be on the inside of the group.

Was he one of the twelve?
Who watched out for him?

There are people in my life, Lord, who seem to be the forgotten ones.
There are those who are shoved aside.
Their needs are neither noticed nor cared for.
There are many disillusioned with the Church,
that they, take Judas' route.
Lord, help me to see the potential Judas' in my life.
Help me to invite others to be involved, and to share their gifts.
Help me to bring your love to them,
so that they may seek a reunion with You and your people.
Lord, may all of us work to make your church
what we are called to be...
Universal...
Catholic and inviting.
Amen.

O, Gentle Heart

O gentle Heart,
that holds mine, too.
I sing of grace
that comes from you.
that comes from love.
that hears my pain,
and then reminds me once again
that all is safe.
Caught in a web of doubt and fear,
you call me forth like Lazarus from his tomb,
and ask for trust while walking near
the freedom road we long for.
Gentle heart,
I thank you from deep within myself,
the holy space where God does dwell
and calls us both to be.
O gentle heart, O healing heart,
O God-drenched heart of mercy.
I cherish you with gratitude.
Amen.

Offering of Self

Jesus,
Crucified One,
Love of my soul,
Path for my life,
your Spirit leads me
here to this desolation
with running streams of new life,
hidden in the recesses of your broken body.
I proclaim you as Lord
of sea and sky,
of desert and abundance,
of valley and mountaintops.
I proclaim you,
as Savior of this world,
and visionary of the Kingdom that is yet to come.
Amen.

On the Cross

Jesus,
arms outstretched,
held by Roman cross and nails,
high above the city of Jerusalem.
The people cry and though
you are engulfed in tears yourself
you hold the people's tears in your heart.

Unselfish Redeemer,
mistreated and misunderstood,
you hang between heaven and earth,
life drawing from you,
yet love flowing forth
to even those who have nailed you to the wood.
Loving Savior,
grace our hearts with forgiveness for others,
as you, in your mercy,
forgive us.

Amen.

For Those Who Lost A Child

Merciful Lord,
the pain of losing a child must be the greatest pain of all.
I have friends who have suffered this loss.
I pray for them and for all women,
that we may be consoled by Mary, Our Mother.
there is a special joy in the anticipation of giving life.
There are hopes and dreams mothers have for their children.
Then, death snatches dreams and leaves sadness
in its place.
Day after day,
memories haunt them,
as they think of what might have been.
Day after day,
they wonder what could have made things different.
Jesus, be their consolation.
Remind us that the children you have called home are now part
of the heavenly angels.
Help us to support those who suffer this loss,
and hold us all in your embrace as you
hold all children.
Help us to believe we will all be together again
in Your heavenly kingdom.
Amen.

For Those Who Have Died

Lord of the Living,
I pray for all those I love who have died.
I know that they are with You,
but sometimes it is so hard to accept.
I miss them, Lord.
I miss their smiles and the sound of their voices.
I miss the good talks we used to have.
I feel sad that our relationship didn't have
a chance to grow deeper.
I know that I should be grateful for the times
we had together…and I am.
But, sometimes, it is so hard to let them go…
to let them be Yours…
Help me, Lord, to let them be Yours… to let
them be at peace in You.
Help me to understand that You loved them so
much that You wanted to enjoy their laughter and smiles.
You wanted to have the pleasure of their company.
In the moments that I feel the loneliest,
help me to imagine what heaven will be like when we
are all together again.
At the times when I really need to speak to them,
help me to know that they are listening
to my words even though we are physically apart.

Jesus, You are the Resurrection.
Give me faith to know that my tears won't be
forever.
Help me to never be ashamed of my tears,
but rather help me to see them as a testimony of
my love for those whom I have loved.

Spirit of Consolation,
be my comfort at the most difficult times of my life.
Hold me tenderly... speak to me gently
and help me to believe that I and my loved ones
are only a prayer apart because we believe in
Jesus.
Amen.

Crucified One

Jesus,
Crucified One.
Life outpoured for love of me.
I sit in your presence,
at your feet Marked with nails.
I watch as you offer yourself for me.
In trembling awe,
I raise my eyes to gaze on You,
to meet you there—vulnerable and open—
to God's will for you.
Lord of All,
God's own son,
you look upon me
as if I am the only one,
and still you remain on the cross
willing to pay the price—
willing to sacrifice.
From your side, the waters rush
to cleanse me, form me,
commission me to do the same,
to give of self without a thought of
cost or pain.

Amen.

A Glimpse of Heaven

Mountain tops, we below
look and see you glorified.
One moment of what will come when
light overtakes the darkness once and for all.
Lord of All,
Giver of Life and Love,
lift me up as you did Moses, Elijah, and Jesus.
Grant to me the promise of good things to come.
May I be for others a moment of
transfiguration,
granting peace and joy to all I encounter.
This is my prayer through
Christ the Lord.
Amen.

Chapter Six

Who is Mary?

Most of us are familiar with the Mary in the Gospel of Luke. She is the young maiden who received a special call from God to become the Mother of the Messiah. The angel Gabriel, a messenger from God, delivered the invitation while Mary was at prayer. Just from this one incident we can deduce that Mary was a woman of prayer. The scripture tells us that Mary was troubled and confused by the words she heard from the angel. She was human, as we are. The scripture also tells us that Mary was willing to listen to the Lord's messenger. Her response to God was YES! She was willing to trust her Lord and God.

Mary's journey through the scriptures shows us a woman of many emotions. When Simeon held her child in the temple, she was warned that her heart would be pierced by who he was meant to be. The Holy Family experienced fear and frustration when the child was lost at the age of twelve. They found him in the temple speaking with the elders. After Jesus left to begin his ministry, his return home was something less than a comfortable visit. Jesus upset the people in the temple when he claimed that the prophecy of Isaiah was being fulfilled. He had to flee for his life. We can only imagine what Mary felt when confronted by neighbors and townspeople. And, of course, Mary walked the road to Calvary with her son.

So, who is Mary? Mary is a woman of prayer. Mary is a Listener. Mary is obedient to God's call. Mary is a person who hears the word of God and acts on it. Mary is compliant to God's will. Mary is genuine in her love and concern for her son.

As Jesus hung on the cross, he gave his mother to us. If we come to know her and love her, we will realize what a gift that is to us. Mary can, and will, intercede for her children. That includes us all.

Mother Mary

Mother Mary,
you hold the redeemer of the world in your arms.
I ask for your protection this day.
Wrap your mantle of love around me as you do for your child.
Mother of the unselfish YES,
given to God through the Angel Gabriel,
help me to ask for the courage
to let my yes grow in my heart.
May I live my life for Jesus as you did.
May I love others as you taught Jesus to love.
My heart is grateful for all
that you have done for me in the past and
I praise God for choosing you to be the Mother of His Son.
Amen.

Mary in the Garden

Lord Jesus, You spoke Mary's name in the garden
and each time she heard you call, she was challenged to believe.
She was challenged to accept your love.
In return, you demanded nothing less than
fidelity of the deepest kind.

Lord Jesus,
You speak my name each time I am in prayer.
If I listen, I can hear your love speaking to me
through the Word and the Eucharist.
I want to recognize your voice.
Fashion my heart to be a listening heart, so that I may recognize You.
Like Mary, let me long to touch you and be with you.
Like Mary, give me the grace to be faithful to you.
Like Mary, make me a witness to your Resurrection.
Amen.

Who is My Mother?

It was a hot afternoon
when you received the word.
Jesus was coming to town.
Your heart leapt with joy!
It had been a long time since his last visit.
You went to the town square where Jesus was.
You sent a messenger to let him know you were there.
"Who is my mother?"
Jesus looked around the crowd.
"These who hear the word of God are my mother and brothers."
You were hurt.

Sometimes, our children say words that hurt.
Help us, Mary, to be like you.
Help us to know that our children do not belong to us.
They belong to God.
Give us the courage to let them go
be as God meant them to be
and find their place in His world.
God is the one who sustains.
Amen.

Sorrowful Mary, Playful Jesus

I gaze upon your image.
A look of sorrow on your face
as Jesus, the Child,
reaches around your neck and tickles.
His shoe hanging from his foot,
perhaps from kicking you,
reminding you that all will be well.

Mary,
come to all mothers who are in need of
consolation and care.
Bring their needs to Jesus, your son.
Let the light-heartedness that Jesus brings you
be a gift to all of us as well.
Mary,
Mother of us all,
be with us.
Amen.

A Mother's Pierced Heart

Mary,
you were told long ago a sword would pierce your heart.
Watching your child go out into the world,
you trusted that God would watch over him.
Today, I pray for all mothers and their children.
I pray for those who are separated by hurt and misunderstanding.
I ask that you surround them all
with your mantle of mercy and love.
Pray for all of us, and ask your Son
to watch over all of us.
Open all hearts to love possible with God as the center.
Be mother to us as you were to Jesus.
Amen.

The Visitation

When you heard the word,
O Mary,
you took upon yourself and the child within,
the journey to see your cousin Elizabeth.
She was also with child.
The road was difficult and hard.
Yet, your love for her was greater than your fear.
The moment you greeted her
the child within her leapt for joy.
Your unselfishness is a model for us.
Mary,
Open our eyes to the needs of others.
Help us to help all in need of our assistance.
Help us to rejoice with the goodness God shares with others.
Mary,
Mother of the Lord and our Mother,
pray for us.
Amen.

In My Mother's Arms

In my Mother's arms, I am safe.
In my Mother's arms I am held with tenderness.
Mary, Mother of us all,
Let your love and kindness wash over me.
may my heart be pure as your heart.
Let the spirit of your loving Son
find a home in me.
Cover me with the mantle of mercy.
Protect me from all harm.
Fill me with joy as
I offer each day to your Son, Jesus.
Amen.

Mary, the Home Maker

Mary,
keeper of the house,
help me offer all I do today for God.
When I am disgusted by the sight of piled up dishes,
give me patience.
When the dust is so thick it makes me sneeze,
give me patience.
When I wonder how a family can make so much dirty laundry,
help me to think about how you had to take
your clothes to the river for washing.
When I feel all alone in the care of the house,
help me take a deep breath
and ask for your help.
Keeper of the home of Nazareth,
you saw to it that Jesus and Joseph were cared for.
You took time to pray as well.
Help me to take the time to care for myself.
Help me to pray.
And help me to make our house a happy home.
Amen.

Chapter Seven

When Prayers

When we experience a difficult situation, we often turn to prayer. When the world becomes too much for us to bear, we turn to prayer. When we cannot understand the will of God, we turn to prayer. Sometimes, when we are aware of how blessed we are, we turn to prayer.

The beautiful thing about prayer is that whenever we want to, we can turn our hearts to God, and in those moments we can experience the love and tenderness of our God.

When I'm Angry

When I'm angry, Lord,
the whole world seems out of place.
It's not me. It can't be me.
No, I think it's everyone else.
I can't see straight.
I can't think straight.
I can't love.
I can't pray.
The anger swells up inside of me.
It chokes any possible opening of my heart to your spirit.
What can I ask for, Lord, except for you to come to me
and hold me tenderly.
Lead me to a greater awareness of your love and forgiveness.
Then, maybe then,
I will be able to let go of the hurt and frustration.
Maybe I will be able to let go of the ugliness I now harbor in my heart.

Create in me a clean heart. Do what you must do within me.
Give me the strength and courage to do the
internal housecleaning I must do.
Help me create a place for you to dwell.
Then, and only then, will I truly be your servant.
Amen.

When I Cannot Choose the Good

When I cannot choose the good,
when I am afraid of saying no,
when I want to go back to what I once was,
help me, God, to choose the good.

When I am tired of the discipline,
when I want to do what is easy,
when I want to give up,
help me God, to choose the good.

I do not walk alone.
I am not in this alone.
I have the power to rise above
and choose the good.

Come, my angels,
come to my aid.
Holy men and women of God,
help me be strong.
And in this hour of need,
help me to choose the good.
Amen.

When Alzheimer's Steals

She is old.
Sometimes, she knows who I am.
When she doesn't recognize me,
I feel torn inside.
I look into her eyes and I know she is still there.
Somewhere, deep inside, she knows me.
She remembers.
Sometimes, I tell her who I am,
and the glaze in her eyes looks beyond my face.
She looks beyond my presence.
She has stepped out for a while.
Then, something jogs her memory,
and her eyes turn towards me.
She smiles.
She reaches for my hand.
She whispers my name.
Lord, be with her and with me.
Help me to understand that Time is stealing her away from me,
and that I must be grateful
for the moments we have together.
Amen.

When A Siren Blares

Father God, who gives us life and all we need,
give aid to those who are in need of medical assistance.
When I hear a siren,
I think of what I was taught long ago,
to send a Hail Mary to heaven for those in need.
Jesus,
help those who require assistance at this time.
May they have hope and trust that the Father's will is done.
Give compassion to those who are present with them.
Spirit of Life,
give your wisdom and efficiency to the medical personnel.
Guide their hands and hearts to do the best they can for others.
Blessed Trinity,
bound together as one,
help us to remember we are all your children.
Call us to pray for one another.
Amen.

When A Friend Loses A Friend

Compassionate Lord,
Giver of Life,
I heard the sadness in my friend's voice
as she told me of the loss of a longtime friend.
I felt her pain.
I was without words,
feeling like nothing I would say could help the hurt.
Then she spoke of faith and hope and love.
She spoke of your promise of eternal life for her friend and for all of us.
There was a calm that settled over the storm of feelings
that death brings on.
There was a sense of future that overcame the helplessness
that death brings on.
Lord, help me to be there for her
in whatever ways that may be helpful to her.
Compassionate Lord,
give her the courage to walk through the pain of loss
and renew in me the belief that You walk with us and
wait for all of us with open arms.
Amen.

When The Little Things Get to Me

Lord,
Why do I let the little things get to me?
Someone passes my office and doesn't greet me.
Is this reason to be upset?
If I am not informed of something going on,
must I feel left out?
When I am not invited out for lunch with the crowd,
does it necessarily mean that I am ignored or disliked?
These are little things.
The more I hold them inside, the bigger they become.
I ask you, Lord,
for the grace to let things roll off my back.
Help to pray for the people I encounter.
Help me to give them the benefit of the doubt.
Help me to refrain from jumping to conclusions.
In this way, your grace will be enough for me
and I will be comfortable again with myself and with others.
Amen.

When I Cannot Get to Mass

Lord,
I cannot get to Mass today.
There is no way other circumstances
would keep me from the table prayer.
I ask you, Jesus,
come to me.
Be present where I am and spend time with me.
My Eucharistic Lord,
I ask that you come to me in
spiritual communion,
filling me with the grace of your presence.
May I experience the grace of the
worshipping community as I trust they remember me in their prayer.
I cannot get to Eucharist, Lord.
Thank you for coming to me.
Amen.

Chapter Eight

Special Occasions

What makes an occasion special? Is it the event itself? Is it the recognition of certain achievements like a birthday, anniversary, or promotion? Is it a holiday, or a holy day?

What makes an occasion special are the people gathering together to share time together. When a family or group of friends gather, they are making memories and in the process of making memories, memories of days gone by are shared.

An occasion becomes special when love is shared. We ought to have hearts filled with gratitude when we experience this special love. Prayer springs forth from the grateful heart.

A Birthday Prayer

O God of life and love,
we give you praise and glory for the many blessings
you shower upon us.
We thank you for the gift of all creation,
that sings its praise in perfect harmony to you.
We thank you for our five senses that allow us to fully enjoy the
beauties of the world.
We thank you for our friends who keep us honest and happy,
and give us hope when times are rough and hard.
We thank you for the gift of faith
that moves us through the fog and challenges
us to trust when we want to give up.
Today, Lord,
we celebrate life.
Together, with our friends and family.
So we pray:
We ask a special blessing on those celebrating a birthday.
We ask that you bestow numerous blessings on them.
Assure them of your love and grace,
both now and forever.
Amen.

Brother Francis

Lord,
what would you have me do?
The question asked so long ago by you, Francis.
You heard the word speak to your heart.
You worked with your hands in joy to help others.
You ministered to the marginal and outcast lepers of your time.
Your joy in Christ made others want to come to Jesus.
Please ask Jesus to help me,
to follow him as you did.
Help me to love the poor and find God's face in them.
Help me to sing a song of joy with every breath I take
and praise the God of all creation as you did with your life.
Help me to believe that nothing is impossible
if I unite myself with our Lord.
Amen.

Sister Clare

Lady Clare of Assisi,
Francis's little plant,
your love of God overwhelmed the people of your day.
Your love of the Eucharist,
your care for the sick and poor,
moved the hearts of nobles and those less fortunate.
Ask the Lord for me,
to give me the vision to see those who are in need,
and to be present to them.
Help me to share my bread.
Instill in me a deeper love of Jesus in the Eucharist and
help me to know the power in the breaking of the bread.
Amen.

A Prayer to Saint Michael

Archangel Michael,
you defend us in battle against the evil one
who roams our earth trying to destroy
the hearts of all who yearn for the holy.
Protect us from being defeated by depression and fear.
These only take us away from the love of God.
Equip us with the sword of truth,
so that we may cast away the lies and deceit of the dragon of hatred.
Lift our spirits so that we may rise above the self-doubts and
confusion that approach us all in the lonely moments of life.
Help us in these stressful moments to trust God all the more.
Michael, be our safeguard and protect us today and always.
Amen.

A Prayer to Saint Raphael

O Healing Angel, Raphael,
come to my aid and heal me of all the burdens
I am being asked to bear.
If it is not possible to remove them,
then walk with me and help me carry them
with faith and trust in the love of the Divine.
May God, who called you to help our ancestors,
call you to help as I journey towards Life.
Be my healing companion, today and always.
Amen.

A Prayer for Priests

Lord Jesus,
I want to pray for priests today.
I know that you have called them to be your hands and heart.
I know that you have given your Spirit to them
so that they can shepherd the people who are yours.
But, they can't do this alone.
They need You and they need us to hold them in prayer.
Bless them as they spend their energies helping your people.
Be in their words as they console those who are in pain.
Be in their touch as they reach out to all who
need to know you are with them.
Be with them in their prayer and in their times of silence.
Refresh them when they are exhausted by the
many demands placed on them.
Give them the courage to ask for help when they need help.
Help them to allow you to be Lord of their lives of service.
Keep them holy, Lord, and keep them pure
in mind and spirit so that their
offering to you might be a prayer of praise and love.
Be kind to them as they turn to you for strength.
Help me be kind to them, too.
Be mindful of their need to know You are pleased with the
sacrifice of their lives for others.
Bless our priests, Lord Jesus,
and keep them close to your loving heart.
Amen.

Bubbles

Father of all Bubble Blowers,
send your spirit of love to us today.
Free us as your sons and daughters.
Inflate our hearts with love and compassion, forgiveness and openness,
so that we may truly be worthy
to be called your children.
Renew in us the innocence and enthusiasm
that you placed in us as children.
May we wonder again at each new, small miracle we experience in life.
Teach us to rise above that which hurts,
confuses, angers, and abuses our right to happiness.
Hold us tenderly, lovingly, and compassionately
in your arms,
today and always.
Amen.

The Donkey Speaks

He was tired and anxious about finding a room for the night.
His wife rode on my back and I tried not to listen.
But, I was there.
He expressed his concern over suitable lodging
but she said she didn't mind.
She felt safe with him and that's all that mattered.
They both knew that God was on their side.
After numerous refusals, he ended up taking her to a barn.
He got her settled for the night.
I remember the hay was fresh, but he scooted me away
from the manger so that he could have it ready when the time came.
I heard her pain and agony as the child was born.
I saw him hold her during those awful hours.
Then, I heard a cry…
A loud, piercing cry, and I knew her time had come.
His time had come.
The world's time had come.
Jesus was born.
And I was there.

Amen.

A Child

You came as a child and trapped me.
Who can resist the beauty of a little one?
You came as a poor one, engaging my
heart in compassion.
Who can resist the cry of one in need?
You came as dependent and in need yourself.
Who can refuse to hold you in one's heart?

Little, poor and in need,
you come.
You are the Lord of all creation.
Little, poor, and vulnerable, you come and place yourself
in our world that cries out for holiness.
You can teach us all to be holy
so we can be a part of your world.

Come, Little Child.
with the gift of peace in your hand.
Come, Little Child,
and be a part of our journey as we walk in your light.
Child of Light, guide us.
Amen.

Summer Prayer

Creator of all, thank You for summer!
Thank You for the warmth of the sun and the increased daylight.

Thank You for the beauty I see all around me,
and for the opportunity to be outside
and enjoy Your creation.

Thank You for the increased time I have to
be with my friends and family,
and for the more casual pace of
the summer season.

Draw me closer to You this summer.
Teach me how I can pray no matter where I am or what I am doing.
Warm my soul with awareness of Your presence,
and light my path with Your Word and Counsel.
As I enjoy Your creation,
create in me a pure heart and a hunger and thirst for You.
Amen.

For the Children

God of love,
bless the children.
Bless those who come from two parent homes,
where you are always welcomed.
Bless those little ones who come from separated homes,
and are asked to grow up too quickly.
Bless the children who are tired of being adults,
and those deprived of the love and care a child needs.
Bless the children who suffer at the hands of adults
who don't know how to handle their anger.
Bless the children who call to you to be the Mother and the Father,
and who need to know you care for them.
Lord, gather the children into your heart this day,
and be for them the Father, Mother, Lord, and God.
Most of all, be their friend, and give them your peace.
Amen.

God of All Jelly Beans

O God, of all Jelly beans,
may I praise you all of my days.
When black darkness keeps me down,
let the promise of the yellow morning dawn give me peace.
When my body aches and my soul isn't far behind,
help me to be in the pink once again.
When everything looks like death,
Open my eyes to the green growth surrounding me.
When I feel like I can't go on, fill me with the radiant red fire of
Your Holy Spirit.
When I feel alone in my journey,
help me to see the white light of your presence and love.
Fill me with a purple passion for life, Lord,
so I may give witness to your resurrection.
God of All Jelly Beans,
fill my life with color and sweetness,
so that I may praise you all my days.
Amen.

If I Believe in Easter

If I believe in Easter,
every day becomes a day
where darkness is broken
by the light of love.

If I believe in Easter,
every day becomes a day
where to share the Bread of Life
is a celebrated meal with those I love.

If I believe in Easter,
every day that seems to feel
like a Good Friday can still be a day of hope.
I know Easter Sunday will follow.

If I believe in Easter,
every day would be a celebration of
Alleluias!

Lord, help me to believe in Easter.
Amen.

Sowing Seeds

Lord, Creator God,
I never know what seeds I sow,
or what words I say.
What small acts of kindness that I do,
touch the heart and soul of others.
Spirits once imprisoned in sadness
are now set free.
Lord, help me to sow the seeds of love
in ground that may seem rocky or sandy at first.
Let me pray that all hearts will be fertile soil
for the planting of your word within your people.
Give me strength to work for the kingdom,
not counting the cost,
but rather trusting that you will nourish the good seeds
I plant in your love.
Amen.

Feeling Old

Lord,
I am old.
My body feels the cold and my bones
know when a change is coming.
My mind plays jokes on me
selecting what to remember, and what to forget.
I move slowly with my shuffling feet.
But, my heart is young.
I feel your love and energy.
My ears are open to your word.
Give me grace and your strength.
Help me to realize that age doesn't matter.
May all I do,
as limited as it may be,
give glory and praise to you.
Amen.

Remember

I remember the times when my heart felt carefree and young.
I would leap into causes that seemed to be
a way to make the world better.
I remember people who would be so enthusiastic about a project
that I would soon be right in there with them,
working towards a common goal.
I remember, too, Lord, how your Spirit would be there,
guiding and moving us to do good works.
I remember feeling your presence.
I remember all the people that I've worked with in the past.
Some are still here and some are home with you.
I remember their smiles.
Thank you for the gift of memories
that help me realize that I have done some good in this world.
Thank you for my life.
Amen.

New Beginnings

Generous God,
we praise and thank you for another day
of opportunities to serve you and your people.

We thank you for the many gifts you throw our way.
We ask that you help us to grow in appreciation
for all those who walk with us as we journey in this life.
Thank you for those we share life with,
laughter and tears, excitement and times of stress.

Thank you that we do not walk alone,
but rather with the love of your Son
and the guidance of your Holy Spirit.

Be with us on the days when we are busy with many things.

Help us to be as hospitable as Martha,
but also as calm as Mary as we listen to your Son's
words to come and rest in His love.

We ask this in the name of all that is good and holy.
Amen.

Be My Glasses

Lord,
be my glasses.
Bring your vision to my eyes.
Help me to see you in family and friends.
Help me to see you in the stranger.
Help me to look with compassion
on the faces of the poor, the disheveled and the
marginal people who are dismissed so easily.
When evening comes, and I look at my image in the mirror,
Please God,
let it be the face of Jesus that I see.
Amen.

Waiting

I hate waiting, Lord.
Whether it's a call I am waiting for,
a friend who's coming to pick me up.
I hate waiting.
I can't understand why the world can't move
as quickly as I want it to.
Many times I don't have anything that is pressing.
I just don't like wasting time.
Then I think of you, Lord.
You wait for me all the time.
You wait for me to get my act together.
You wait for me to open up to the Holy Spirit.
You wait for me to love those I would rather ignore.
you wait for me and never complain.
Would you send me a touch of your patience, Lord?
Please send it my way.
Maybe I can get used to using the time I wait to talk to you.
Then I won't be wasting time.
I'll be giving that extra time to you.
Thanks for waiting for me.
Amen.

Like Abraham

Like Abraham, you call me.
You call me to an unknown land and people and ask
that I trust you.
So I venture out with your promises ringing
in my ears and heart.
I venture out to find you, the living God of all.
I am frightened by the call.
I am frightened by the journey.
I am frightened by the dark valley and crevices I see.
But, in confidence, I move ahead following
voice so crystal clear within me.

To whom shall I go?
Where does the path lead?
I see your face in all the marvels of creation.
Your handprint on the earth, your breath in the wind
shout your praise.
My name, too, you have written on your palm.
Your hand grasps mine tightly as a parent holds onto
the child.

Like Abraham, you call me.
Like Abraham, may I trust you without fear.

Amen.

One Single Prayer

One single prayer, Lord,
connects me to you and all the holy people
who have followed you.
One single moment of remembrance
brings my heart one step closer to yours.
What a gift you give me, Lord,
in your desire to want to be friends with me.
I am a sinner,
yet you are merciful and kind and you don't hold
my sin against me.
Help me today and every day to utter one single prayer.
I give thanks and praise to you for being
Lord of my life.
Amen.

Making Time

Lord,
You have taught me well that I cannot make time.
There are only 24 hours in a day, and every
day seems to be busier than the last.
I try to make time… for you and for others.
Make time to clean the house.
Make time to organize things I have promised to organize.
I try to make time to bake my favorite recipes.
I try to make time to sit back and relax.
I promise to make time for you, Lord.
But, I cannot make time.
I only have the time you give me,
and I must choose what to do with my time.

Help me, Lord, to make good choices.
Help me to choose life giving adventures that
draw me closer to you and those I love.
Help me to share my time with those in need.
Help me to take time to thank you for all the gifts you give me.

Thank you for the gift of time, Lord.
Help me make the most of the time I have.
Help me understand I will never be able to make time.
Amen.

To Be Young Again

To be young again,
to feel the earth under your feet,
to feel each and every blade of grass,
to be adventurous,
to dare to leap into the waves,
to tease the sea and laugh in its face,
to wiggle sand between your toes,
to write precious words with a stick in hand,
and watch the roaring ocean eat them.

To sit and think and pray,
letting your thoughts ascend beyond your dreams,
feeling free,
to relax and enjoy the goodness about you,
the goodness within.
Free to touch the earth,
to love the earth,
to hug huge rocks,
to lie flat on your back and watch the clouds,
to let the crickets sing their song in your ears,
Letting your soul give praise to the Creator.

To be young again,
to know the God of our youth,
to let our hearts be touched by the One who loves us,
to unite our soul with the Divine,
to enter into the creative process we are all a part of.

To be young.
To know.
To be reborn in love once again.

A Blessing for Pets

Creator of all,
I ask a blessing on my pet.
You give us companions,
who bring us joy and comfort.
Bless these animals with good health
and vitality, so that they can continue to
give you praise and give us enjoyment.
Help us to treat them with respect
and do all we can to keep them healthy and happy.
Thank you for bringing them into my life.
Amen.

When a Pet Dies

Lord,
You created animals to be our loyal companions.
You entrust us to the care of them.
Today, you called my pet home
and sadness fills my heart.
I have memories of all the good times we had together.
I remember times cuddling was so consoling to me.
There were times when my pet was the only friend I had.
Now my pet is gone,
and there is emptiness in my heart.
Sit with me as I remember
and give me a grateful heart as I remember the gift my pet was.
Thank you for the times we had together.
Thank you for the love we shared.
Amen.

Can We Talk?

Creator of All,
can we talk?
I want to know why things are so tense in our world.
I want to know why it is so hard for us to live in peace together.
I begin my day wanting to make a difference.
I am easily discouraged when I hear the news.
I hate seeing people making violence a way of life.
Isn't there any good news?
I need some help, here.
I need you to show me a little bit of hope.
Open my eyes to the good around me.
Use me, if you will.
I want to make a difference.
You created a world in beauty and harmony.
Teach us all what we must do to return such a world back to you.
Amen.

A Grandparent's Prayer

Lord,
You gave me the gift of children.
You have extended this gift by giving me grandchildren.
I ask that you send your angels to guard and protect these precious gifts.
I thank you for the joy they bring me.
I thank you for the silliness they bring out of me.
I thank you for the hugs and kisses and especially for the snuggles
when I need them most.
I am blessed.

I hope that our being together instills in them a love for life.
I hope they remember me when I am gone, and all the fun times.
May they grow to love you, Lord, above all.
Thank you for these special signs of hope.
I pray they will make a difference in our world.
Amen.

What Others are Saying about

Prayers

No Experience Necessary

Jo Therese can place on paper what many of us long to say to our loving God each day. Through her own experiences and deep spiritual devotion, *Prayers* will become a well-read companion on your own spiritual journey. These prayers will provide comfort, hope and peace for both private and community prayer times. We love to share them at our staff meetings and there always seems to be a perfect one just for our gathering!

Michelle Zakula
Director of Pastoral Care
St. Gregory the Great Parish
Milwaukee, Wisconsin

We are familiar with prayer finding voice in our communal experience as the hymnal or order of worship comes to life through our throats. We cherish those prayers we learned at some time in our life that find their voice in our memories. The Our Father, Hail Mary, Glory Be are prayers that sometimes lose their beauty in the automatic reciting. Then there are those very special prayers that are locked away, written in our hearts by God's own hand as we experience life in all its many expressions and feelings. So often they do not find a voice. This gathering of heart felt prayers may touch a cord, may give you a sense of someone in a similar journey to your own…but their greatest power is in their giving your own heart the encouragement and permission to find its voice for your own prayers.

Deacon James Banach
Saint Gregory the Great Parish
Milwaukee, Wisconsin

Jo Therese's PRAYERS for all life situations seems quite logical: God manifests God's self in each situation of life. Jo Therese's work, the fruit of many close encounters in her life and relation to God and the things of God, is inspiration for my prayer life. The call is to "pray always" in all circumstances. Thank you, Jo Therese, for this many-splendored gift for our faith life.

-Sister Helen Weier,O.S.C. Author
Monastery of St. Clare
Bloomington, Minnesota

As a recovering alcoholic and being sober for over 22 years, I try to find peace and serenity. Each day at different times I read short prayers. I found Prayers very helpful. Some of them even brought tears to my eyes. Thank you so much for your spiritual journey and writing such beautiful prayers. God bless.

Mark Kurzynski
Director of Maintenance
St. Gregory the Great Parish
Milwaukee, Wisconsin

About the Author

JO THERESE FAHRES grew up in Milwaukee, Wisconsin. Her spirituality over the years has been flavored especially through the charisms of St. Francis and St. Clare of Assisi. Jo Therese's struggle with faith in the Catholic Church began when she was studying at Cardinal Stritch University in Milwaukee.

Daily trips to the grassy lawns in the back of the college introduced her to the beauty of creation as seen through the eyes of St. Francis. As she read and studied the struggles of Francis and Clare, she could identify with their journey of trying to find God. Her seven years as a Franciscan religious rooted her in a grass-roots spirituality which has been a deep part of her life. Her prayers come from the realization that God is a mystery and is revealed every day to the heart that is open.

Jo Therese has worked in church ministry for over forty years. She holds a Bachelor's of Arts degree in Art Education and Religious Studies and a Master's Degree in Religious Studies from Cardinal Stritch University. She has written *Thinning with the Angels*, the story of her journey toward truth about addiction. With faith in God and the angelic assistance that God provides to all human beings, Jo Therese was able to walk through dark periods of despair and find hope again. She has also written for *Children Celebrate*, a program of Pflaum Publishing Group that share the Sunday Scripture readings with children. She currently serves as Director of Child Ministry at Saint Gregory the Great Catholic Church, where she has worked for the past twenty nine years. Jo Therese has served as Spiritual Director for Third Order Lay Franciscans Groups. She facilitates days of prayer and reflection. She has taught both elementary and high school art and theology in the Archdiocese of Milwaukee.

Jo Therese holds a Bachelor of Arts degree in Art Education and Religious Studies and a Master's Degree in Religious Studies from Cardinal Stritch University in Milwaukee. She also studied at the Franciscan Institute of St. Bonaventure's University in New York.

Jo Therese has been married to her husband Jerry for 34 years. They are the proud parents of two adults, Anthony and Therese, and the proud grandparents of Clare, Oliver and Rose.